ZOMBIES READ GRAPHS!

BY THERESE M. SHEA

Gareth Stevens
PUBLISHING

Please visit our website, www.garethstevens.com. For a free color catalog of all
our high-quality books, call toll free 1-800-542-2595 or fax 1-877-542-2596.

Library of Congress Cataloging-in-Publication Data

Names: Shea, Therese, author.
Title: Zombies read graphs! / Therese M. Shea.
Description: New York : Gareth Stevens Publishing, [2019] | Series: Monsters
  do math! | Includes bibliographical references and index.
Identifiers: LCCN 2018024194| ISBN 9781538229385 (library bound) | ISBN
  9781538233061 (pbk.) | ISBN 9781538233078 (6 pack)
Subjects: LCSH: Graphic methods--Juvenile literature. | Mathematics--Graphic
  methods--Juvenile literature. | Zombies--Juvenile literature.
Classification: LCC QA90 .S51246 2019 | DDC 511/.5--dc23
LC record available at https://lccn.loc.gov/2018024194

First Edition

Published in 2019 by
Gareth Stevens Publishing
111 East 14th Street, Suite 349
New York, NY 10003

Designer: Sarah Liddell
Editor: Kate Light
Illustrator: Bobby Griffiths

Photo credits: pp. 4, 7, 9 (zombies) TroobaDoor/Shutterstock.com; p. 5 leolintang/
Shutterstock.com; p. 6 chaiyapruek youprasert/Shutterstock.com; p. 20 Elena
Elisseeva/Shutterstock.com; p. 21 Alastair Rae/Josve05a/Wikimedia Commons.

Printed in the United States of America

CPSIA compliance information: Batch #CW19GS: For further information contact Gareth Stevens, New York, New York at 1-800-542-2595.

CONTENTS

Words in the glossary appear in **bold** type the first time they are used in the text.

HUNGRY FOR GRAPHS!

You hear groaning outside. You look out the window and see people walking oddly toward your home. But they don't look like any people you've ever seen. Their skin is rotting off! They're zombies!

Don't worry! They're not hungry for brains. These zombies are here to help you understand **graphs.** Graphs will be helpful for keeping track of more dangerous zombies in your neighborhood. Check your answers to the questions in this book with the answer key on page 22.

ZOMBIES ARE POPULAR CREATURES IN MANY BOOKS, MOVIES, AND TV SHOWS TODAY.

PICTURING THE UNDEAD

You might make a graph to record the number of zombies in your neighborhood and where you see them. That way, you'll know which places to avoid!

Sometimes comparing amounts on a graph is easier than reading about facts and figures, or data. A picture graph uses pictures to **represent** data.

MONSTER FACTS!

TALES OF ZOMBIES MAY COME FROM VOODOO, A **RELIGION** OFTEN PRACTICED IN HAITI. SOME PEOPLE WHO BELIEVE IN VOODOO THINK THAT DEAD PEOPLE CAN BE BROUGHT BACK TO LIFE AND FORCED TO WORK.

NUMBER OF ZOMBIES ON EACH STREET

Look at the picture graph above. To understand what it's telling you, read the title and the labels on the sides. The key tells you how many zombies each picture represents.

Use the graph to answer these questions: Where are the most zombies? Where are the fewest zombies?

7

SPOT THE ZOMBIE

To live through a zombie **invasion**, you'll need a team of zombie spotters. Gather a group of friends and get to work. Just don't let the zombies spot you!

MONSTER FACTS!
ZOMBIES ARE SOMETIMES CALLED THE UNDEAD. THEY'RE NOT QUITE DEAD BECAUSE THEY MOVE AROUND—BUT THEY'RE NOT QUITE ALIVE EITHER!

Use the picture graph below to answer these questions: How many zombies did Charlotte spot? How many zombies did Cam spot? How many more zombies did Cam spot than Charlotte? Be sure to check the key before you answer!

NUMBER OF ZOMBIES SPOTTED

 = 2 ZOMBIES

NUMBER OF ZOMBIES

AVA   MARK   CHARLOTTE   CAM

ZOMBIE SPOTTER

SUPER ZOMBIES!

Bar graphs use bars or blocks to show amounts. They're a good way to show how many zombies in your neighborhood have certain powers! Some of the zombies are strong but slow. Others are really fast. Still others have super strength and speed!

MONSTER FACTS!
SOME ZOMBIES HAVE ROTTING SKIN. IN OTHER STORIES, ZOMBIES MADE BY MAGIC MAY HAVE **PRESERVED** BODIES.

ZOMBIE POWERS

NUMBER OF ZOMBIES

20
18
16
14
12
10
8
6
4
2

STRENGTH   SPEED   STRENGTH AND SPEED

POWERS

To read the bar graph above, match the top of each bar with the number it lines up with on the left. Use the graph to answer these questions: How many zombies have only speed? How many zombies have both strength and speed?

BARRING THE WAY

A bar graph can show data about how the people in your neighborhood are protecting, or guarding, their homes from super-powered zombies!

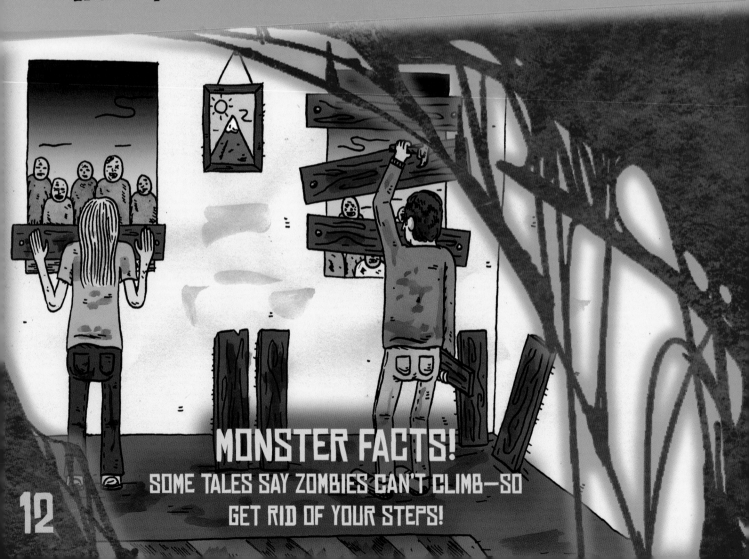

MONSTER FACTS!
SOME TALES SAY ZOMBIES CAN'T CLIMB—SO GET RID OF YOUR STEPS!

Use the bar graph below to answer these questions: How many neighbors protected their homes by boarding up the windows? Which zombie protection method did the fewest neighbors use?

KEEPING ZOMBIES OUT

STEEL DOORS	
BOARDED-UP WINDOWS	
TALL FENCES	
NO FRONT STEPS	

5   10   15   20   25   30

NUMBER OF NEIGHBORS

CHANGING NUMBERS

Sometimes data changes over time. Line graphs are a great way to show these changes. You might need to see if the number of zombies in your neighborhood is growing!

MONSTER FACTS!

ZOMBIES USUALLY AREN'T SMART CREATURES. INSTEAD, THEY'RE CONTROLLED BY SOMEONE—OR BY THE NEED TO EAT BRAINS!

NUMBER OF ZOMBIES THROUGH THE WEEK

NUMBER OF ZOMBIES

20
19
18
17
16
15
14
13
12
11
10
9
8
7
6
5
4
3
2
1

MONDAY   TUESDAY   WEDNESDAY   THURSDAY   FRIDAY   SATURDAY   SUNDAY

DAY OF THE WEEK

Use the line graph to answer these questions: Does the graph tell you that the number of zombies is rising or falling over time? How many more zombies were seen on Sunday than on Monday?

15

BAD BITERS

The number of zombies in your neighborhood could be increasing because they're **infecting** people and making them into zombies, too! Zombies usually spread infection by biting people.

MONSTER FACTS!
IN SOME STORIES, SCIENTISTS TRY TO FIND A CURE FOR THE ZOMBIE INFECTION.

NUMBER OF ZOMBIE BITES

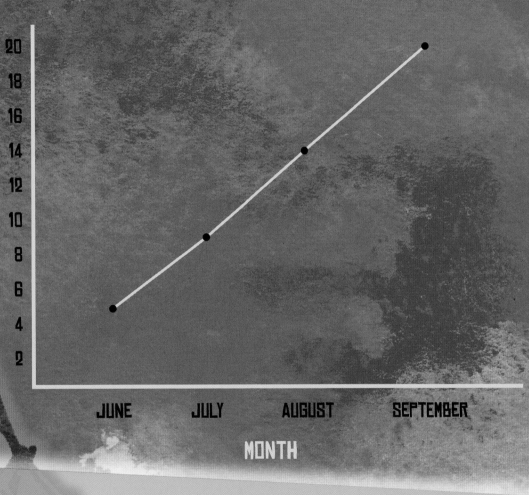

NUMBER OF BITES REPORTED

20
18
16
14
12
10
8
6
4
2

JUNE   JULY   AUGUST   SEPTEMBER

MONTH

This line graph shows data about zombie bites during the summer in your neighborhood. Use it to answer this question: How many more bites were reported in September than in August?

17

FIGHTING BACK

You don't want the zombie invasion in your neighborhood to spread. That might lead to the zombie **apocalypse**! After showing your graphs to the government, they ask you and your neighbors to stay in **quarantine**—with the zombies!—until they can find a cure for the infection.

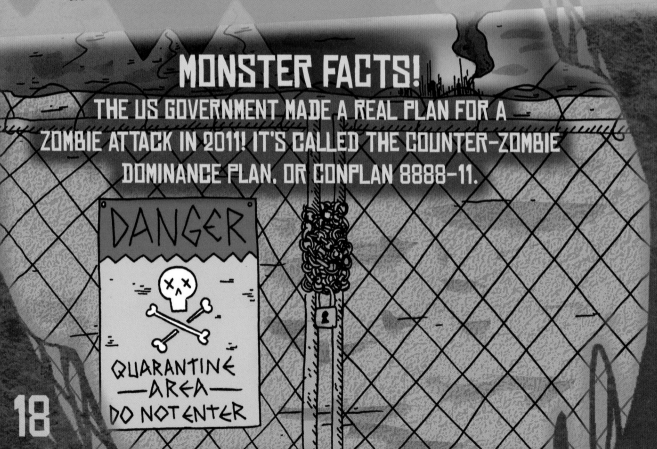

MONSTER FACTS!

THE US GOVERNMENT MADE A REAL PLAN FOR A ZOMBIE ATTACK IN 2011! IT'S CALLED THE COUNTER-ZOMBIE DOMINANCE PLAN, OR CONPLAN 8888-11.

DANGER

QUARANTINE
—AREA—
DO NOT ENTER

The pie graph below shows facts about everyone in quarantine. The whole graph represents the total number. Each slice of the pie represents a part, or a fraction, of the whole.

WHO'S IN QUARANTINE?

PEOPLE BITTEN BY A ZOMBIE

ZOMBIES

PEOPLE WITHOUT ZOMBIE INFECTION

What fraction of those in quarantine doesn't have the zombie infection, 1/2 or 1/4?

SAVED BY MATH!

Scientists found a cure! The dangerous zombies are gone, and all your bitten neighbors are healthy again. By using graphs, you spotted the zombie problem and proved it was getting worse. You used the graphs to get help. That means you and your graphs saved your neighborhood!

Graphs are helpful for recording the results of all sorts of research. You can use them for your next monster hunt. You can use math to save the world!

ZOMBIES AREN'T ONLY IN STORIES. SOME ANIMALS CAN TURN OTHER ANIMALS INTO ZOMBIELIKE CREATURES! FOR EXAMPLE, HAIRWORMS MAKE GRASSHOPPERS TAKE THEM TO WATER.

21

GLOSSARY

apocalypse: the end or destruction of the world

graph: a drawing that uses dots, lines, or other symbols to show how much or how quickly something changes

infect: to cause someone to become sick with an infection, or an illness caused by germs that enter the body

invasion: the entry of a force into an area in order to take control of it

preserve: to keep something in its original state

quarantine: the state of being kept away from others to stop an illness from spreading

religion: a belief in and way of honoring a god or gods

represent: to stand for

ANSWER KEY

page 7: most zombies on Grape Avenue; fewest on Main Street

page 9: 2 zombies; 4 zombies; Cam spotted 2 more zombies than Charlotte.

page 11: 10 zombies with speed; 6 zombies with strength and speed

page 13: 25 neighbors boarded up their windows; steel doors

page 15: rising; 8 more zombies

page 17: 6 more bites

page 19: 1/2

FOR MORE INFORMATION

BOOKS

Gosman, Gillian. *Graph It: Reading Charts and Graphs.* New York, NY: PowerKids Press, 2015.

Hamby, Rachel. *How to Read Graphs.* North Mankato, MN: Child's World, 2018.

Knudsen, Shannon. *I'm Undead and Hungry! Meet a Zombie.* Minneapolis, MN: Millbrook Press, 2015.

WEBSITES

Data Graphs (Bar, Line, Dot, Pie, Histogram)
www.mathsisfun.com/data/data-graph.php
Visit this site and try making your own graph.

Graphs
www.ixl.com/math/graphs
Answer questions about different kinds of graphs here.

INDEX